Cooking With Mama Joyce: The One-Handed Chef
Authored by Joyce A. Graham

Copyright © 2024 by Joyce A. Graham

All rights reserved. Printed in the United States of America. No part of this book may be used or reproduced in any manner without written permission except in the case of brief quotations embodied in critical articles used in structured cooking lessons.

Library of Congress Cataloging-in-Publication Data is available upon request.

The Library of Congress
United States Copyright Office
101 Independence Ave., S.E.
Washington, D.C. 20559-6000
202-707-3000

Cover Design by Joyce A. Graham
Cover Graphics by Mithun Miah
Photography by Meghan I. Rogers
Consultation by Toneal M. Jackson, APS Publishing Company
Published by Back to the Basics Ministries

ISBN-13:9798876446336
BISAC: Comfort Food/Soul Food/Southern Cuisine

Cooking with Mama Joyce
"The one-handed Chef"

Over 50 Soul-food recipes that taste just like Mama used to make.

Also by Joyce A. Graham

In Search of Hope

Back to the Basics

Succession: Mentoring the Next Generation

Surviving Transition

Still Searching...

Mental Health Issues in the 21st Century Church

Disclaimer:

I believe that it is safe to say that not one recipe in the 21st century is original. I am not discounting creativity or authenticity while cooking in the kitchen, but no one was born automatically knowing how to cook.

I am 70 years old and in all my years of cooking, I have tweaked hundreds of recipes handed down to me by my mama and other great cooks who were kind enough to share their recipes and cooking prowess with me. Those recipes were most likely handed down to them and tweaked as well.

Someone has undoubtedly shared a recipe with you or you saw it in a cook book. Or perhaps you viewed a demonstration of a dish being prepared during a cooking show on television, Face Book, YouTube, etc. So if you recognize an ingredient, recipe or a cooking technique that looks familiar in this cookbook, please know that I am sharing my own personal version. I share these recipes with you because I want to encourage you to get back into the kitchen and cook!

Never hesitate to share your recipes with others for fear that they will lose their value. But please know that once you do, more than likely it will be duplicated and/or tweaked! Consider it as a compliment! Happy Cooking!

With His Love,
Mama Joyce

*"Cook for a person and they eat for a day;
give them the recipe and they eat for a lifetime..."*
~*Joyce A. Graham*~

Table of Contents

Dedication
Acknowledgements
Introduction

Chapter 1	Meats	**18**
Chapter 2	Vegetables	**42**
Chapter 3	Soups & Salads	**59**
Chapter 4	One-Pot Meals & Casseroles	**78**
Chapter 5	Desserts	**93**
Chapter 6	Breads	**108**
Chapter 7	Miscellaneous	**123**

Appendix A: Conversion Measurement Chart
Appendix B: Stick of Butter Conversions
Appendix C: Cooking Tools for the Handicapped
Appendix D: Helpful Cooking Tips

Dedication

I dedicate this book:

To those of you who have had an illness or an injury that has impaired your ability to cook and you want to get back into the kitchen...

Acknowledgements

I would like to acknowledge all of the amazing cooks in my life who have shared their delicious recipes with me and who have greatly influenced my own, personal cooking style:

My mama, **Rosa Lee Edmond**
My grandma, **Lucille Harris**
My sisters, **Myrtle L. Humphrey** & **Rosetta Watts**

My personal Taste Testers/Food Critics:
My husband, **Carl T. Graham, Sr.**
My sister, **Dorothy J. Greer-Brown**

Introduction

On March 23, 2020, I suffered a massive stroke which left the entire left side of my body paralyzed. Later that same year in November, I contracted Covid-19 which further immobilized me.

After over 4 years of intense physical and occupational therapy, I eventually learned to take limited steps with the use of a quad cane. However, for the most part, I was confined to a wheelchair.

My husband, Carl and my granddaughter, Meghan became my primary caregivers, but there was only one problem; Carl could not cook and Meghan could only prepare limited, simple dishes.

For the first year of my illness and confinement, my older Sisters, Myrtle and Rosetta along with some of the women from our church prepared delicious, home cooked meals for us. On the days that they were not available, we ate fast food.

I began to crave those good ole home cooked, soul food dishes that I used to prepare before the stroke and Covid. I have always considered myself a fairly decent cook and the kitchen had always been my "Happy Place."

One day I felt inspired and strong enough to prepare a simple breakfast consisting of only toast and cereal. It was very difficult to accomplish this from my wheelchair using only the one hand that was functional. However, during my time in rehab therapy, I had learned how to compensate for the functions that I no longer had.

When Meghan saw me struggling in the kitchen, she went to Amazon online and discovered that there were cooking aids available for handicapped people who had physical limitations like me. She purchased a cutting board, a food chopper, a vegetable peeler, a rocker knife, and a can and jar opener, all that could be operated safely and were specifically designed for people like myself who only had the use of one hand or were confined to food preparation from a wheel chair. My husband also purchased an air fryer and an instant pot, making food preparation a lot easier and quicker. (Please refer to pages 142 and 143 for an illustration of those items).

Eventually, I began to tackle more complex, challenging recipes, such as fried chicken, pork chops, and fish. Soon, I moved on to more complicated dishes, like cornbread dressing, pot roasts, chili, soup and collard greens. I even advanced to baking desserts like cakes and pies.

When I was in therapy, the constant mantra was "SAFETY FIRST!" So in the beginning of being back in the kitchen, I was never alone nor unsupervised. If I needed help with lifting heavy pots or taking something hot out of the oven, Carl and Meghan were always on hand to assist me. I can truly say that cooking has been therapeutic for me and, once again, the kitchen is my "Happy Place!"

I want to encourage those of you who have had an illness or an injury that has impaired your ability to cook and you want to get back in the kitchen again, to, first of all, get clearance from your doctor or your therapist; then start out with something simple before advancing to more complicated dishes.

Remember these three things:

#1 Always PRAY before you begin

#2 Ask for HELP when you need it

#3 SAFETY FIRST!

With the help of God and by His grace, you can do this!

With His Love,
Mama Joyce

Chapter 1

Meats

Fried Chicken

Ingredients:

8-10 various chicken pieces
Salt
Black Pepper
Onion Powder
Lawry's Seasoned Salt
2 cups Flour (For Dredging)
Vegetable Oil

Directions:

Soak chicken for 10-15 minutes in cool water to which 3 caps of apple cider vinegar has been added.

Thoroughly rinse chicken in clear cool water, pat dry, and place in a bowl. Season lightly with salt and black pepper and set aside.

In a separate, large bowl combine 2 cups of flour, 2 teaspoons Lawry's Seasoned Salt, 1 teaspoon black pepper, and 1 teaspoon onion powder. Mix well.

Using a deep frying pan, add enough vegetable oil that will adequately cover chicken, but not to where it will spill over.

Heat vegetable oil until it is hot but not burning.

Dredge chicken pieces in the flour mixture.

Carefully add chicken in batches, frying each batch until the chicken is golden brown on all sides.

Drain the chicken on a cooling rack or paper towels.

Smothered Chicken

Ingredients:

Follow recipe for fried chicken on Page 20.
Follow the recipe for Gravy on Page34 or Page 127

Fried chicken pieces
1 medium Onion (chopped)
½ Bell Pepper (chopped)
2-3 stalks of Celery (chopped)
Chives or parsley for garnish

Directions:

Start by frying the chicken according to the directions on Page 20. Set the chicken aside while you make your gravy following the recipe on Page 34 or Page 127. Be sure to make enough gravy to cover your chicken as it simmers.

Place the chicken in the gravy, turn the heat on low, and cover the pan, (Add the onions, celery, and bell peppers at this time if you so desire to add more flavor).
Let the chicken, onions, celery, and bell peppers simmer for 20-25 minutes until tender, stirring occasionally in the middle so that the meat does not stick. After the chicken is done, you may garnish it with chives or parsley.

*Note: This same exact recipe can be used for smothered pork chops.

Fried Pork Chops

Ingredients:

4- 6 bone in pork chops
Salt
Black Pepper
Onion Powder
Lawry's Seasoned Salt
2 cups Flour (For Dredging)
Vegetable Oil

Directions:

Soak pork chops for 10-15 minutes in cool water to which 3 caps of apple cider vinegar has been added.

Thoroughly rinse pork chops in clear cool water, pat dry, and place in a bowl.

Season lightly with salt and black pepper and set aside.

In a separate, large bowl combine 2 cups of flour, 2 teaspoons Lawry's Seasoned Salt, 1 teaspoon black pepper, and 1 teaspoon onion powder. Mix well.

Using a frying pan, add enough vegetable oil to completely cover the bottom of the pan.

Heat vegetable oil until it is hot but not burning.

Dredge the pork chops in the flour mixture.

Carefully add the pork chops in batches, frying each batch until the pork chops are golden brown on both sides.

Drain the pork chops on a cooling rack or paper towels.

Meatloaf

Ingredients:

2 pounds of ground chuck
1 package Lipton Beefy Onion Soup Mix
½ sleeve of crackers, crushed
1/2 medium onion, diced
1/3 medium bell pepper, diced
Black Pepper
Onion Powder
Garlic Powder
2 eggs, beaten

Directions:

Preheat the oven to 350 degrees.

In a large bowl, add the meat, Lipton Beefy Onion Soup Mix, crushed crackers, onions, bell peppers, 1-2 teaspoons black pepper, 1 teaspoon onion powder, 1 teaspoon garlic powder, and the beaten eggs.

Mix well until all ingredients are combined. DO NOT OVER MIX.

Form meat into a loaf and place it in a pan.

Bake the meatloaf, uncovered, for 45-60 minutes. Check the meatloaf to make sure that it is cooked through. This will all depend on the size and shape of your meatloaf.

When the meatloaf is done, let it cool for at least 10 minutes before slicing.

If you desire gravy, follow the directions on Page 34 or Page 127.

Fried Cat Fish

Ingredients:

4- 6 cat fish fillets
Salt
Black Pepper
Onion Powder
Lawry's Seasoned Salt
Yellow or White Cornmeal
Vegetable Oil

Directions:

Soak fish in cool water for 10-15 minutes.

Thoroughly rinse fish in clear cool water, pat dry, place in a bowl, season lightly with salt and black pepper and set aside.

In a separate, large bowl combine 2 cups of Cornmeal, 2 teaspoons Lawry's Season Salt, 1 teaspoon Black Pepper, and 1 teaspoon onion powder. Mix well.

Using a deep frying pan, add enough vegetable oil that will adequately cover fish, but not to where it will spill over.

Heat vegetable oil until it is hot but not burning.

Dredge fish pieces in the cornmeal mixture.

Carefully add fish in batches, frying each batch until fish is golden brown on all sides.

Drain fish on a cooling rack or paper towels.

*Note: You can use this exact same recipe for all types of fish that fry well, including: buffalo, flounder, perch, red snapper, tilapia, etc.

Cornish Hens or Baked Chicken

Ingredients:

1-2 Cornish hens or 1 Regular Hen
Butter
Vegetable oil
Lawry's Seasoned Salt
Paprika
Black Pepper
Onion powder
Garlic powder
Onions (rough chopped)
Green pepper (rough chopped)
Celery (rough chopped)
Chicken broth
Slurry of 3 tablespoons corn starch in 2 cups of water

Directions:

Preheat the oven to 350 degrees.

Remove giblets from the hen(s).

Wash the hen(s) and pat dry

Melt the butter and combine it with the vegetable oil.

Brush the hen(s) liberally with the melted butter and oil mixture.

Season the hen(s) with all seasonings.
Stuff the hen(s) cavity with onions, green pepper, celery, and butter.

Add vegetables in a bed in an oven safe pan.
Lay hen(s) on top and tuck the wings.

Add slurry around the perimeter of pan being careful not to remove seasoning.

Cover the pan with aluminum foil.
Bake at 350 for 45 minutes
Remove the foil and base the hen(s).

Let the hen(s) brown uncovered for approximately 15-20 minutes.

Smothered Turkey Wings

Ingredients:

3-4 pounds turkey wings
(Optional): split into flats and drums
Butter
Vegetable Oil
Paprika
Garlic Powder
Onion Powder
Salt
Sage
Black Pepper
1 large yellow onion (sliced)
1 medium green bell pepper (sliced)
3 stalks celery (rough chopped)

Directions:

Preheat oven to 350F.

Soak turkey wings for 10-15 minutes in cool water to which 3 caps of apple cider vinegar has been added.

Thoroughly rinse the turkey wings in clear cool water, pat dry, and place them in a roasting pan.

Melt the butter and combine it with the vegetable oil.

Drizzle the wings with the melted butter and oil mixture.

In a small bowl, mix 2 teaspoons salt, 2 teaspoons black pepper, 1 teaspoon sage, 1 tablespoon paprika, 1 tablespoon garlic powder, and 1 tablespoon onion powder. Sprinkle the seasonings over the wings making sure to cover both sides.

Top the wings with the sliced onions, sliced bell peppers, chopped celery and cover with foil. Bake for 1 hour and 15 minutes.

Uncover the pan and set oven on broil.
Bake the wings uncovered for 35-45 more minutes or until they are golden brown. Do not allow the wings to become dry or the drippings to dissolve.

After removing the pan from the oven, pour the drippings in a cup and save for making the gravy. Follow directions for gravy on Page 34 or Page 127.

Ingredients for gravy:

½-1 stick of butter or ¼ cup of vegetable oil
¼ cup flour
1 teaspoon garlic powder
1 teaspoon onion powder
1 teaspoon salt
1 teaspoon black pepper
1 medium onion (chopped)
Turkey Broth, Chicken Broth, or Pan Drippings.

Directions for gravy:

Heat the butter or vegetable oil in a large skillet over medium heat. Once butter or oil is hot, add the onions into the skillet. Cook until the onions are soft.
Then stir in the garlic powder, onion powder, salt, black pepper. Cook for 1-2 more minutes.

Slowly and carefully add the flour a little at a time while constantly whisking. Keep whisking until the flour is the color you desire.

Gradually whisk in the turkey broth, chicken broth or pan drippings.

Keep adding and whisking in the broth or pan drippings until you achieve the thickness you desire. (Continuous whisking will prevent lumps).

Remove the pan from heat, taste and adjust your seasoning.

Pot Roast

Ingredients:

3-5 pound Chuck roast
1 large yellow onion peeled and quartered
4 garlic cloves peeled
6-8 baby carrots cut in half
4 Yukon gold potatoes quartered
Onion powder
Garlic powder
Lawry's Seasoned salt
Black pepper
1/4 cup vegetable oil
1/2 cup Beef broth
1/2 cup water
2 tablespoons Worcestershire sauce
1/2 cup Flour for dredging roast

Directions:

Preheat oven to 350F.

Wash the roast and pat dry.

Season the meat liberally with all seasonings on both sides and dredge in the flour.

Pour 1/4 cup vegetable oil in a skillet and heat over medium heat.

Add the roast and sear on both sides until golden brown.

Place the roast in a roasting pan.

In a small bowl, mix together 1/2 cup of beef broth, 1/2 cup water, and 2 tablespoons Worcestershire Sauce.

Pour this mixture around the perimeters of the pan.

Add the onions, garlic cloves, carrots and potatoes on top of the roast. Cover the pot with a lid or aluminum foil.

Place the pan in the oven for 2 1/2 to 3 hours or until fork tender (more time may be needed depending on how large the roast is).

Let the roast rest after removing it from the oven and before slicing.

Neck Bones and Potatoes

Ingredients:

4-6 Pork Neck bones
4 Yukon Gold Potatoes (quartered)
1 large onion (chopped)
2 teaspoons Lawry's Seasoned Salt
2 teaspoons black pepper,
2 teaspoons onion powder
2 teaspoons garlic powder
1 packet of Lipton Beefy Onion Soup mix

Directions:

Clean and wash the neck bones thoroughly.

Soak the neck bones for 10-15 minutes in cool water to which 3 caps of apple cider vinegar has been added.

Rinse under cold water and drain.

In a large pot, add all seasonings and enough water to cover the neck bones. Bring the pot to a rapid boil, then reduce heat, cover pot and cook for 1 hour.

After 1 hour add the packet of Lipton beefy onion soup mix. Cook for an additional hour.

Then add the chopped potatoes and the chopped onion. Bring to a boil. Then reduce heat and let simmer until everything is tender.

Oven Barbecue Ribs

Ingredients:

2 Racks of Spare Ribs (about 10 lbs.)
Garlic Powder
Onion Powder
Black Pepper
Lawry's Seasoned Salt

Directions:

Preheat the oven to 300°F.

Remove the membrane (the silver skin) from the back of the ribs. Wash ribs thoroughly under cool running water. Pat dry.

Season the ribs liberally with Lawry's Seasoned Salt, black pepper, garlic powder and onion powder.

Place the ribs on an aluminum foil lined baking sheet. (For easy cleanup.) Cover tightly and completely with an additional top layer of foil.

Bake at 300°F for 2-3 hours. You'll know they are done when the meat begins to fall off the bone.

Remove from the oven, uncover and brush with your favorite barbecue sauce.

Leave uncovered and return the ribs the oven. Set the oven on broil and broil at 475°F for a few additional minutes to get a delicious crust on the top. You can also finish them on an outdoor grill.

41

Chapter 2
Vegetables

Asparagus

Ingredients:

1 pound fresh asparagus spears
1/4 stick butter
1/4 cup olive oil
1 teaspoon Salt
1 teaspoon Black Pepper
1/2 teaspoon Garlic Powder
1/2 teaspoon Onion Powder

Directions:

Cut off the tough ends of the asparagus. You can also cut the spears in half if you want smaller pieces which will also cook faster.

Rinse well under cool water
Mix the butter and olive oil and heat the mixture in a large skillet over medium heat.

Place asparagus in the skillet and add all seasonings. Gently stir the asparagus to coat all of the spears with the seasonings and the butter and olive oil mixture.

Cover the skillet and lower heat
Allow the asparagus to cook until they reach the tenderness and texture that you desire. Do not overcook them or allow them to become mushy.

A light sprinkle of Parmesan cheese, crushed red pepper or bacon bits for extra flavor and garnishing is optional.

Broccoli

Ingredients:

Several heads of broccoli (chopped)
3 tablespoons water
1/2 stick of butter (cubed)
1 teaspoon salt
1/2 teaspoon black pepper

Directions:

Place chopped broccoli in a microwave-safe bowl and pour 3 tablespoons of water over the top.

Add the cubed butter, salt and black pepper. Cover and microwave on high for 2 to 4 minutes, until broccoli is tender.

Carefully remove, uncover and garnish with bacon bits.

Smothered Cabbage

Ingredients:

1 medium cabbage
1 medium onion
1 small bell pepper
6 strips of bacon
¼ cup chicken broth
1/2 stick of butter
1 teaspoon salt
1 teaspoon black pepper

Directions:

Remove the thick outer leaves and the hard center core of the cabbage.

Chop the remaining cabbage into bite sized, uniform pieces. Wash in cold water, drain well and set aside.

Rough chop the onion and green bell pepper and set aside.

Cut the 6 pieces of bacon into bite sized, uniform pieces.
Fry the bacon until it becomes crisp.

Remove the bacon and set it aside.

Place the cabbage, onion and bell pepper, into the fat rendered from the bacon.
Add the chicken broth and the butter on top of the vegetables. Add the salt and black pepper.

(You may have to add the cabbage in batches, adding more as the previous addition wilts depending on the size of your skillet.)

Cover the skillet and cook over medium heat, stirring occasionally, until the cabbage reaches the tenderness and texture that you desire.

Taste and adjust seasoning.

Transfer the cabbage to a serving dish and garnish it with the crispy bacon pieces that were left.

Mixed Greens and Ham Hocks

Ingredients:

2 - 3 medium smoked ham hocks
1 lb of fresh turnip greens
1 lb of fresh mustard greens
1/4 - 1/2 cup of bacon drippings
Black pepper
Salt
Garlic Powder
Onion Powder
2 chicken bouillon cubes

Directions:

Remove stems from the greens, chop, and wash thoroughly in cold water. Drain the greens of all water and set aside.

Soak the ham hocks in cold water to which a little apple cider vinegar has been added for 15 minutes

Rinse the ham hocks and let them drain.

In a large pot place the ham hocks and enough water to cover them and bring to a boil. Add a little black pepper, salt, onion powder and garlic powder.

Reduce heat to slow boil and cook for 1 and 1/2 hours.

Remove the ham hocks from the pot and set aside. Add the 2 chicken bouillon cubes to the pot and allow them to dissolve.

Add the first batch of greens to the pot.

Season the first batch of greens with black pepper and half of the bacon drippings.

After they have cooked down, add a second batch of greens.

Season the second batch of greens with black pepper and the remaining bacon drippings.

After all the greens have been added, add the ham hocks back to the pot and cook until the ham hocks and greens are tender.

Taste and correct seasonings as necessary

*Hint: Be careful not to add too much water. Greens make their own liquid.

Green Beans and Potatoes

Ingredients:

1 lb. frozen or fresh green beans
4-6 strips thick, smoked Bacon (chopped)
3 medium Yukon gold potatoes (quartered)
1 medium onion (chopped)
½ teaspoon salt
1 teaspoon Black Pepper
1 teaspoon Onion powder
1 teaspoon Garlic Powder
1/2 stick butter
2-4 cups Vegetable or Chicken Broth

Directions:

Sauté the bacon over medium heat until the bacon starts to render drippings.

Then add the chopped onions and sauté until the onions are translucent.

In a medium pot add the broth, butter and seasonings.

Add the potatoes and the green beans. Cover and reduce the heat to medium-low. Cook covered for about 20 minutes or until potatoes and green beans are tender, stirring occasionally.

After 20 minutes, add the bacon, onions and bacon drippings. Cover and continue cooking for an additional 5-10 minutes.

Remove from the heat, taste and add additional seasoning if needed.

Collard Greens, Ham Hocks and Turnip Bottoms

Ingredients:

2 lbs of fresh collard greens
2 - 3 medium smoked ham hocks
2 medium turnip bottoms (peeled and quartered).
1/4 to 1/2 cup of bacon drippings
Black pepper
Salt
1 teaspoon Garlic powder
1 teaspoon Onion powder
2 chicken bouillon cubes

Directions:

Remove stems from the greens, chop, and wash thoroughly in cold water. Drain greens of all water and set aside.

Soak the ham hocks in cold water to which a little apple cider vinegar has been added for 15 minutes

Rinse ham hocks and let them drain.

In a large pot place the ham hocks and enough water to cover them and bring to a boil. Add a little black pepper, salt, onion powder and garlic powder.

Reduce heat to slow boil and cook for 1 and 1/2 hours.

Remove the ham hocks from the pot and set aside. Add the 2 chicken bouillon cubes to the pot and allow them to dissolve.

Add the first batch of greens to the pot.

Season the first batch of greens with black pepper and half of the bacon drippings.

After they have cooked down, add a second batch of greens.

Season the second batch of greens with black pepper and the remaining bacon drippings.

After all greens have been added, add the ham hocks back to the pot. Then add the turnip bottoms and allow to cook until the ham hocks, greens, and turnip bottoms are tender.

Taste and correct seasonings as necessary

*Hint: Be careful not to add too much water. Greens make their own liquid.

Candied Yams

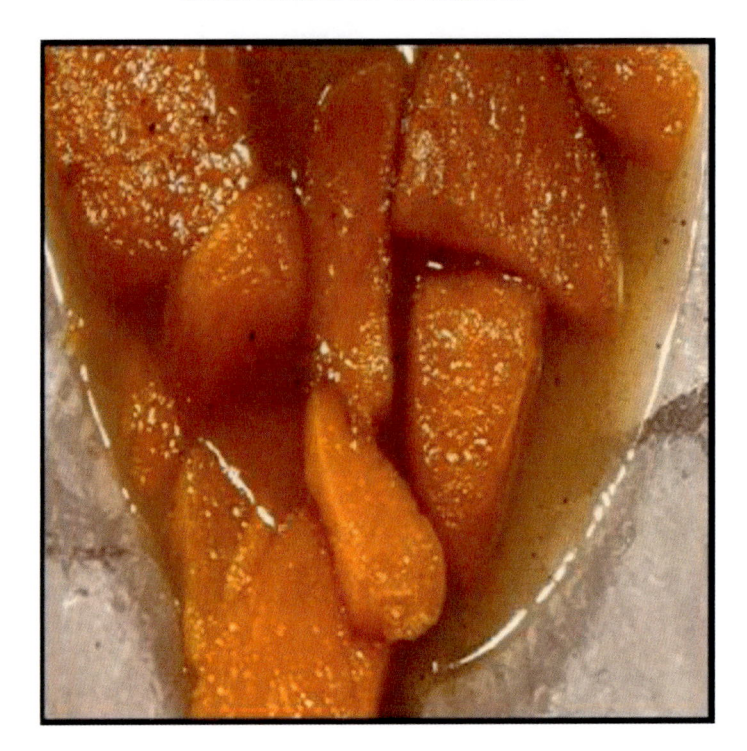

Ingredients:

4 medium sized sweet potatoes
1 cup white sugar
1/2 cup light brown sugar
1 teaspoon nutmeg
1/4 teaspoon salt
1 stick butter
2 teaspoons vanilla extract

Directions:

In a medium sized bowl add the white sugar, light brown sugar, salt and nutmeg. Stir until combined.

Cut, peel, and slice the potatoes into 1/4 inch pieces.

Add just enough water to cover the bottom of a large pot and set on stove top. Turn on the stove to medium high.

Add a first layer of half of the potatoes into the pot. Cover potatoes with 1/2 of the white sugar, light brown sugar, salt and nutmeg mixture. Next cut up and add 1/2 stick of the butter. Add 1 teaspoon vanilla.

Add the last layer of potatoes. Cover potatoes with the remaining white sugar, light brown sugar, salt and nutmeg mixture. Cut up and add the remaining butter. Add 1 teaspoon vanilla.

Bring pot to a low boil then reduce heat and cover pot with a tight fitting lid. Cook for approximately 15-20 minutes or until the potatoes are tender.

Remove lid and continue cooking while periodically gently folding the potatoes until all of the potatoes are covered in a glossy, sweet syrup. Be careful while stirring so that the potatoes are not mashed or broken up.

Chapter 3

Soups & Salads

Vegetable Beef Soup

Ingredients:
1 pound ground beef or ground chuck
2 fresh potatoes (chopped in bite sized pieces)
2 fresh carrots (chopped in bite sized pieces)
1/2 medium onion (chopped)
1/3 green pepper (chopped)
1 stalk of celery (chopped)
1 package frozen vegetables
1 small can of corn, peas, & string beans
1 small can of diced tomatoes
1/2 (24 oz. jar) of Prego Traditional tomato sauce
1/2 stick butter
2 tablespoons vegetable oil
Beef Broth
1 beef bouillon cube
Salt
Black pepper
Sugar
Lawry's Seasoned Salt
Onion powder
Garlic powder

Directions:

Sauté chopped onions, chopped bell pepper, and chopped celery in a skillet with the combined melted butter and oil.

Season them with a little salt and black pepper
Add the meat to same skillet and season with a little Lawry's Seasoned Salt, onion powder, garlic powder, and black pepper.
Let meat brown until it is no longer pink.
Drain and set aside

Drain all canned vegetables (with the exception of the canned tomatoes) and set aside.

Add 3 cups beef broth and 4 cups of water to a separate pot.

Add the potatoes, carrots, and beef bouillon cube to the pot. Cook until the potatoes and carrots are tender.

Then add the sautéed onions, green peppers, celery, drained meat, the can of diced tomatoes, the Prego Spaghetti sauce, frozen vegetables, and the drained canned vegetables.

Season entire pot with:

3-4 teaspoons sugar

1 teaspoon salt

1 to 2 teaspoons black pepper

Let simmer for 30-45 minutes.

Vegetable Soup

Ingredients:

2 fresh potatoes (chopped in bite sized pieces)
2 fresh carrots (chopped in bite sized pieces)
1/2 medium onion (chopped)
1/3 green pepper (chopped)
1 stalk of celery (chopped)
1 package frozen vegetables
1 small can of corn, peas, & string beans
1 small can of diced tomatoes
1/2 (24 oz. jar) of Prego Traditional Tomato Sauce
1/2 stick butter
2 tablespoons of vegetable oil
Beef Broth
1 beef bouillon cube
Salt
Black pepper
Sugar

Directions:

Sauté chopped onions, chopped bell pepper, and chopped celery in a skillet with the combined melted butter and oil.

Season them with a little salt and black pepper.

Drain all canned vegetables (with the exception of the canned tomatoes) and set aside.

Add 3 cups beef broth and 4 cups of water to a medium pot.

Add the potatoes, carrots, and beef bouillon cube to the pot.

Cook until the potatoes and carrots are tender.

Then add the sautéed onions, green peppers, celery, the can of diced tomatoes, the Prego Traditional Tomato Sauce, frozen vegetables, and the drained canned vegetables.

Season entire pot with:

3-4 teaspoons sugar

1 teaspoon salt

1 to 2 teaspoons black pepper

Let simmer for 30-45 minutes

Chicken Noodle Soup

Ingredients:

1 Rotisserie Chicken (cut into pieces)
1/2 bell pepper
1 medium Onion
2 stalks celery
1 teaspoon onion powder
1 teaspoon garlic powder
2 teaspoons black pepper
2 chicken bouillon cubes
1/2 stick of butter
1/2 pack extra wide egg noodles

Directions:

Cut up chicken and place in a pot with 6 quarts of water.

Add all vegetables, seasonings, butter and bouillon cubes.

Allow to come to a boil. Lower heat. Allow to cook until chicken is tender.

After chicken is tender, add 1/2 pack of egg noodles and cook until noodles are desired tenderness.

Garden Salad

Ingredients:

1 head of lettuce
1 small bag of baby spinach
1 cup cherry tomatoes (halved)
1 cucumber (sliced)
8 oz. Cheddar cheese (shredded)
1 medium shallot (chopped)
1/3 medium green bell pepper (diced)
1 carrot (shredded)
Salt and black pepper to taste
1 cup of Salad dressing of your choice

Directions:

Place chopped lettuce into a large bowl.

Add all ingredients.

Add salt, and black pepper to taste.

Add dressing and toss to coat.

Chef Salad

Ingredients:

1 head of lettuce (chopped)
8 oz Deli ham, chicken, and/or turkey (diced)
1 cup Cherry tomatoes (halved)
1 medium cucumber (sliced)
1 medium shallot (diced)
8 oz. Cheddar cheese (cubed)
4 large Hard Boiled Eggs (diced)
Salt and black pepper to taste
1 cup buttermilk ranch dressing
Bacon Bits for garnishing

Directions:

Place chopped lettuce into a large bowl.

Add ham, chicken, and/or turkey, tomatoes, cucumbers, cheese, onions, diced eggs, salt, and black pepper.

Add dressing and toss to coat.

Garnish with bacon bits.

Tuna Salad

Ingredients:

4 six ounce cans of tuna in olive oil
4 boiled eggs (diced)
1/3 jar of sweet pickled relish
4 teaspoons of sugar
1 and 1/2 teaspoons of salt
2 teaspoons of black pepper
3 tablespoons of miracle whip
½ red Onion
1/3 bell pepper
1 stalk of chopped celery

Directions:

Drain tuna of all oil
Put drained tuna in a medium sized mixing bowl
Add diced eggs, onions, bell pepper, and celery to bowl.
Add salt, black pepper, and sugar.
Lightly stir mixture.
Add pickle relish and miracle whip
Mix until combined.
Refrigerate for approximately ½ hour.
Garnish with paprika and parsley.

*Note: You can use this recipe for similar types of salads that contain protein, including: chicken salad, egg salad and turkey salad. Just swap out the protein.

Potato Salad

Ingredients:

4 medium Russet Potatoes
4 boiled eggs (diced)
1/3 jar of sweet pickled relish
4 teaspoons of sugar
1 and 1/2 teaspoon of salt
2 teaspoons of black pepper
3 tablespoons of miracle whip
½ Red Onion (diced)
1/3 bell pepper (diced)

Directions:

Peel and cut potatoes in bite sized pieces.
Boil potatoes until tender, but not mushy.
Drain and put potatoes in a bowl.
Add diced eggs, onions, and bell pepper to the bowl with potatoes. Add salt, black pepper, and sugar.
Gently stir mixture. Add pickle relish and miracle whip. Mix until combined.

Refrigerate for approximately ½ hour

Garnish with paprika and parsley

Tomato, Cucumber and Onion Salad

Ingredients:

1 cup Cherry tomatoes (halved)
1 medium cucumber
1 small red onion (diced)
2 tablespoons olive oil
1 tablespoon apple cider vinegar
Salt, black pepper and sugar to taste

Directions:

Start by washing the tomatoes and cucumber. Cut the tomatoes in half and cut the cucumber into slices.

In a bowl, combine the tomatoes, cucumbers, and onions.

In a small bowl, mix together the olive oil, apple cider vinegar, salt, black pepper and sugar.

Pour the dressing over the vegetables and toss.

Garnish with bacon bits if desired.

Chapter 4

One-Pot Meals & Casseroles

Beef Stroganoff

Ingredients:

1 16 oz. Package of extra wide egg noodles
1/4 cup butter
1 pound leftover chuck roast (cubed)
Salt
Black Pepper
1 medium onion (chopped)
1 1/2 cups beef stock
1 tablespoon Worcestershire Sauce
1/4 cup of corn starch

Directions:

Cook noodles according to package instructions, drain and set aside.

Sauté the onions in the butter. After onions are translucent, add the cubed chuck roast. Season with salt and black pepper.

In a separate pot, add the beef stock and the Worcestershire sauce. After the liquid is hot, lower the heat and whisk in the corn starch until mixture is smooth. Add the onions and meat to the pot.

Finally, add the noodles and gently fold until all ingredients are well combined, careful not to tear noodles. Taste and season with additional salt and black pepper if needed.

Mac N Cheese

Ingredients:

2 cups elbow macaroni
1/2 stick butter
1 can evaporated milk
1/2 cup of Velveeta Cheese (cubed)
1 cup Cheddar Cheese (shredded)
1 teaspoon salt
1/2 teaspoon black pepper
1/4 teaspoon sugar
Parsley Flakes

Directions:

Cook macaroni according to instructions on the package.

Drain and set aside (do not rinse).

In a separate medium sized pot, add the evaporated milk, 1/2 stick of butter, 1/2 cup of shredded cheddar cheese, 1/2 cup of Velveeta cheese, 1 teaspoon salt, 1/2 teaspoon black pepper, and 1/4 teaspoon sugar. Cook over low heat until cheese is melted and all ingredients are incorporated.

Add drained macaroni to the pot and gently fold until everything is combined.

Pour entire mixture into a buttered casserole dish, cover and bake at 325° for 15 to 20 minutes.

Uncover and sprinkle top completely with remaining shredded cheddar cheese. Turn oven on low broil and broil until cheese has melted and is golden brown. Lightly garnish the top with parsley flakes.

Chili

Ingredients:

1 lb. ground beef or ground turkey
1 chili brick
1 40 oz. can of Brooks Chili Hot Beans
1 14 oz. can of petite diced tomatoes
1 medium onion (chopped)
1/3 green bell pepper (chopped)
Vegetable oil
1 pkg. Williams Original Chili Seasoning
Garlic powder
Onion powder
Chili powder
Ground cumin
Lawry's Seasoned Salt
Salt
Black pepper
Sugar
Cayenne Pepper (optional)

Directions:

Put chopped onion and chopped bell pepper in a skillet to which 2-3 tablespoons of vegetable oil has been added. Season the onions and bell pepper with a little salt and black pepper and sauté until soft.

Add the ground meat and the chili brick to the skillet with the onions and bell pepper.

After the meat has browned and drained of any excess oil, add the following:
1 teaspoon garlic powder
1 teaspoon onion powder
2 teaspoons Lawry's seasoned salt
2 teaspoons black pepper
Add the entire packet of Williams Original Chili Seasoning along with 1 cup of water.
 Stir and let simmer for about 5 minutes.

In a separate pot add canned tomatoes and chili beans. Heat until hot then pour skillet of sautéed onions, bell peppers, drained ground meat and chili brick mixture into the pot.

Finally, season the entire pot with:
3 teaspoons of Cumin
3 teaspoons of Chili powder
3 teaspoons of Black pepper
4 teaspoons of sugar
1 teaspoon salt
Optional: Add 1 teaspoon of cayenne pepper if you want that extra hot kick.

Mix and stir well. Let pot simmer on low for at least 20-30 minutes stirring every 10 minutes or so.

Cornbread Dressing

Ingredients:
1 pan of cornbread (You may follow the recipe on Page 112).
1 sleeve of Saltine crackers
4 pieces of dark toast
4 stalks of celery, diced
1 yellow onion, diced
1/2 green bell pepper, diced
Sage
Salt
Black Pepper
Chicken Broth
1 stick of butter
2 eggs (beaten)

Directions:

Crumble the cornbread, crackers and toast in a large bowl. Sautee onions, green peppers, and celery in 1 stick of butter seasoned with a little salt and black pepper until translucent Then add them to the bowl.

Then add the following to the bowl:
1 teaspoon of black pepper
1 teaspoon of salt
1 teaspoon of sage

Add enough broth for a creamy consistency.
Add the 2 beaten eggs to the mixture LAST.
Mix well and pour mixture into a buttered, casserole baking dish.

Cover the dish with foil and bake at 350 degrees for 45 minute to 1 hour.

Remove foil and turn oven on a low broil to brown.
(Do not allow dressing to get dry).

Spaghetti

Ingredients:

1 pound ground beef or ground chuck
3/4 package of a 16 oz. box of thin spaghetti
2 (24 oz.) jars of Prego Traditional Sauce
1/2 medium onion (chopped)
1/3 medium bell pepper (chopped)
Garlic powder
Onion powder
Salt
Black Pepper
Lawry's Seasoned salt
Sugar
1/2 stick of butter

Directions:

Sauté chopped vegetables in 1/2 stick of butter seasoned with a little salt and black pepper. Sauté vegetables until they are translucent.
Add meat to skillet. Brown and season with a little of the following seasonings:
Onion Powder
Garlic Powder
Lawry's Seasoned Salt
Black Pepper
Cook spaghetti in a separate pot until tender. Spaghetti should be tender, but not mushy. Drain the spaghetti and return it to the pot.
Add meat mixture to the drained spaghetti.
Add 1 and ½ jars of Prego traditional sauce
Add a cup of water if more liquid is needed.

Finally, season the entire pot with the following:
3-4 teaspoons sugar
3 teaspoons garlic powder
1 teaspoon salt
1-2 teaspoons black pepper
Let simmer for 10-15 minutes (Gently fold spaghetti frequently and do not allow it to stick to bottom of the pot or burn)

Mostaccioli

Ingredients:

16 oz. package Mostaccioli
1/2 pound ground beef
1/2 pound pork or Italian sausage
1 and 1/2 jars of Prego Traditional Sauce
1/2 onion (chopped)
1/3 bell pepper (chopped)
Garlic powder
Onion powder
Salt
Sugar
Black Pepper
Lawry's Seasoned Salt
1/2 stick of butter
Shredded Mozzarella cheese
Shredded Cheddar cheese
Parmesan cheese
Parsley flakes

Directions:

Preheat the oven to 350°F. In a large pot of salted water, boil Mostaccioli noodles until al dente according to package directions. Drain and set aside.

Sauté vegetables in 1/2 stick of butter and seasoned with a little salt and black pepper. Sauté vegetables until they are translucent. Add ground chuck and sausage to the skillet. Brown and season meat with a little of each:
Onion Powder
Garlic Powder
Lawry's Seasoned Salt
Black pepper

Return the mostaccioli to the pot and add meat sauce mixture.
Add 1 and 1/2 jar of Prego Traditional Sauce
Add a little less than a jar of water if needed.
Season entire pot with:
3-4 teaspoons sugar
3 teaspoons garlic
1 and 1/2 teaspoons salt
2 teaspoons Black Pepper
Let simmer

Assemble:
In a buttered 9x13 deep casserole dish place a bottom layer of mostaccioli/meat mixture. Then add a layer of shredded mozzarella and shredded cheddar cheese. Follow with another layer of the mostaccioli/meat mixture. Top with a final layer of shredded cheddar cheese.

Cover the mostaccioli with foil, place in the oven and cook for 30 minutes. Then uncover and switch the oven to low broil, and broil for 3-5 minutes, watching closely so the cheese doesn't burn.

Remove from the oven and top with parsley and/or Parmesan. Let casserole rest for at least 15 minutes before serving.

Chapter 5
Desserts

Sweet Potato Pie

Ingredients:

4 medium sweet potatoes
1 stick of butter
1/4 cup pet milk
2 eggs (beaten)
1/4 teaspoon salt
1 cup sugar
1/4 cup flour
1 teaspoon nutmeg
1 teaspoon vanilla extract
1/2 teaspoon lemon extract
2 regular pie shells

Directions:

Roast the potatoes in the oven until tender. Let potatoes cool.

After potatoes have cooled, peel and then mash them in a large bowl.

Add the remaining ingredients to the bowl and blend well until everything is combined.

Pour the mixture into the pie crusts and bake at 350 degrees for a little over 1 hour.

Allow pies to cool before cutting.

Banana Pudding

Ingredients:

3 cups whole milk
3 tablespoons cornstarch
1/4 teaspoon salt
1 cup sugar
4 egg yolks (save the egg whites for making the meringue)
1 tablespoon butter
2 teaspoons vanilla extract
60 Vanilla wafers
3 bananas, thinly sliced

Directions:

In a small bowl, whisk together ¼ cup of the milk with the cornstarch. Set aside.

In a medium saucepan, whisk together the remaining milk, salt, and sugar. Heat the mixture over medium heat until it is steaming, do not let it boil.

While the milk heats, whisk the egg yolks in a separate small bowl. Once the milk is steaming, slowly stream ½ cup of the hot milk mixture into the egg yolks, whisking constantly.

Slowly add the egg yolk mixture back to the pot, followed by the cornstarch mixture. (This is called tempering) Continue to cook over medium heat, whisking constantly, until the mixture starts to simmer and has thickened.

Remove from the heat and whisk in the butter and vanilla.

Let the mixture cool, cover it with plastic wrap, place it in the refrigerator and allow it to chill for several hours.

Banana Pudding Assembly:

Cover the bottom of an oven safe casserole dish with Vanilla wafers. Arrange half of the banana slices over the Vanilla wafers. Pour half of the pudding mixture over the bananas. Repeat layers.

If you wish to cover the top of your pudding with meringue, follow the directions on Page 99.

Meringue Ingredients:

4 egg whites
1/4 teaspoon cream of tartar
6 tablespoons granulated sugar
1/2 teaspoon vanilla extract

Meringue Directions:

To make the meringue, beat the egg whites and cream of tartar with an electric mixer until foamy. Gradually add sugar and keep beating on high speed until stiff peaks begin to form. Mix in the vanilla extract.

Spread the meringue on the top of banana pudding, being sure to completely cover the pudding. Bake until the meringue is golden brown.

Ebony and Ivory Cake

Ingredients:

2 cups of cake flour
3 teaspoons baking powder
1/4 teaspoon salt
1 ½ cups sugar
½ cup butter
3 eggs
1 cup milk
1 teaspoon vanilla extract

Directions:

Preheat the oven to 350 degrees F.
Grease and flour 2 cake pans.

Combine flour, baking powder, and salt together in a medium bowl.

Cream sugar and butter together in a large bowl with an electric mixer until light and fluffy. Add eggs, one at a time, beating thoroughly after each addition. Add flour mixture alternating with milk, beating just enough to combine. Stir in vanilla and pour cake batter into the prepared pans.

Bake in the preheated oven until a toothpick inserted in the center comes out clean, about 30 to 35 minutes. Cool cakes completely and top with ½ vanilla frosting topped with coconuts and ½ with chocolate frosting. Follow the directions for chocolate frosting on Page 106.

Pound Cake

Ingredients:

3 cups cake flour
3 cups sugar
3 sticks butter
6 eggs
1/4 teaspoon salt
1 teaspoon baking powder
1 (3.4 oz. pkg.) instant vanilla pudding
2 teaspoons vanilla
2 teaspoons butter extract
1 teaspoon lemon extract
1 cup buttermilk

Directions:

Preheat oven to 325 F
(Set buttermilk and eggs out to become room temperature).

Prepare a 12-15 cup tube pan by spraying it generously with Bakers Joy, Pam or by coating it with butter and flour.

Cream butter until light and fluffy. Gradually add sugar and continue to cream until mixture resembles ice cream.
Add eggs one at a time just until combined.

In a separate bowl, mix dry ingredients (flour, salt, pudding and baking powder)
Add all flavoring extracts to the cup of butter milk and stir
Add (fold) in 1/3 of the dry ingredients into the butter, egg, and sugar mixture.
Then add (fold) in 1/2 of the milk.
Add (fold) in half of remaining dry ingredients.
Then add (fold) in the rest of the milk
Finally add (fold) in the remainder of the dry ingredients.

Pour the batter into the prepared pan.
Bake at 325 degree oven for 1 hour. Cake is done when a skewer inserted in the middle of the cake comes out clean with only a few crumbs attached). If cake is not done, bake an additional 10-15 minutes, checking for doneness at 5 minute intervals. Bake until skewer inserted in the middle of the cake comes out clean with only a few crumbs attached.

Allow the cake to cool for exactly 10 minutes on a cooling rack before inverting.

Chocolate Cake

Ingredients:

2 cups flour
1 cup Cocoa Powder
1 teaspoon baking powder
1 teaspoon baking soda
1 cup sugar
½ cup packed light brown sugar
2 teaspoons salt
2 large eggs
½ cup vegetable oil
1 cup buttermilk
1 teaspoon vanilla extract

Directions:

Preheat oven to 350°F. Lightly grease and flour two cake pans

Sift flour, cocoa, baking powder and baking soda into a large bowl. Add both sugars and salt and whisk to blend well, pressing out any lumps of brown sugar.

Combine eggs, oil, buttermilk and vanilla in a medium bowl and whisk to blend well. Pour into the bowl with the dry ingredients and mix with an electric hand mixer on medium-low until blended.

Divide batter evenly between the prepared pans and bake for 30-35 minutes until cakes spring back when pressed gently and a skewer inserted into the center comes out clean. Transfer pans to a wire rack and let cool for 15 minutes before inverting.

Frosting Ingredients:

8 oz. dark chocolate coarsely chopped
1 cup whipping cream
2 tablespoons light syrup
2 tablespoons cocoa powder
½ cup sour cream

Frosting Directions:

Combine chocolate, whipping cream and syrup in a saucepan over low heat and stir until completely melted, smooth and glossy.

Pour mixture into a bowl and whisk in cocoa powder. Add sour cream and whisk it through so it is evenly combined.

Let the mixture cool for 15 minutes.

Use the frosting immediately, covering the cooled cake layers.

Chapter 6
Breads

Yeast Rolls

Ingredients:

3 and ¼ cups flour, divided
1 packet of dry active yeast
1 and ¼ cups milk
1/4 cup sugar
1/4 cup of butter flavored shortening
1 egg
1 teaspoon salt

Directions:

Preheat oven to 400 F degrees

In a large bowl, add 1 and 1/4 cup of the flour and the yeast. Mix with a whisk until combined then set aside.

In a saucepan, over medium heat, add milk, sugar and shortening. Stir constantly until shortening has melted. Do not boil. Let the mixture cool for a bit before pouring the milk mixture into the flour/yeast mixture.

Add in the egg.

Beat on low speed for 1 minute and then on high speed for 3 minutes.

Add in the salt and the rest of the remaining 2 cups of flour. Mix lightly by hand until a soft ball of dough begins to form.

Grease a separate bowl with vegetable oil and place the ball of dough in it. Cover and refrigerate it for at least 2 hours.

Remove from refrigerator and punch down the dough with your fist to release the air.

Spread a thin layer of melted butter in the bottom of a 9 X 13 pan.

Take a chunk of dough and form it into your desired roll shape.

After forming each roll, place them into the buttered pan and brush a little butter on each one.

Cover the pan with a thin kitchen towel and let it sit in a warm place for at least 1-1 ½ hours.
Put the pan of rolls in the oven and bake for 10-15 minutes or until light golden brown.

When they come out of the oven brush them on top with a little butter.

Cornbread

Ingredients:

1 and 1/2 cups yellow cornmeal
1/2 cup Martha White self rising cornmeal
2 tablespoons sugar
2 teaspoons baking powder
1/2 teaspoon baking soda
1/4 teaspoon salt
1 and 1/2 cups buttermilk
2 large eggs
1 stick melted butter

Directions:

In a medium sized bowl, combine these dry ingredients:
1 and 1/2 cups yellow cornmeal
1/2 cup Martha white self rising cornmeal
2 tablespoons sugar
2 teaspoons baking powder
1/2 teaspoon baking soda
1/4 teaspoon salt

In a separate medium sized bowl, combine these wet ingredients:
1 and 1/2 cups buttermilk
2 large eggs
1 stick melted butter

Mix dry and wet ingredients in a large bowl.

Stir until ingredients are mixed well.

Pour into a well greased pan.

Bake in a 400 degree oven for 20-25 minutes.

Brown on low broil if necessary.

Hot-Water Cornbread

Ingredients:

2 cups yellow cornmeal
1/2 teaspoon salt
1 tablespoon sugar
2 tablespoons melted butter
1/2 cup vegetable oil
1 and 1/2 cups boiling water

Directions:

Mix cornmeal, salt, sugar, and melted butter in a large bowl. Then add the boiling water. Thoroughly mix until the cornbread mixture is smooth.

Heat 1/2 cup vegetable oil in a cast iron skillet or frying pan over medium-high heat.

Scoop up about three tablespoons of batter into the palm of your hand. Flatten, then gently drop it into the oil.

Keep dropping patties into the pan without over crowding or overlapping.

Fry each batch of patties until golden brown and crisp; turn with a spatula, and then brown the other side.

Drain the patties on a cooling rack on paper towels.

Buttermilk Biscuits

Ingredients:

1/2 tsp salt
4 teaspoons sugar
2 1/2 teaspoons baking powder
1 cup cold Crisco butter flavored shortening
1 cup buttermilk
2 cups flour
1 stick melted butter

Directions:

In a large mixing bowl stir together flour, baking powder, sugar and salt. Using a pastry blender, cut in shortening until mixture resembles coarse crumbs.

Make a well in the center of the flour mixture. Add the cup of buttermilk. Using a fork, stir just until moistened and dough pulls away from the sides of the bowl (dough will be sticky).

On a floured surface, lightly knead dough with floured hands for 30 seconds or until almost smooth. Lightly roll dough to 3/4-inch thickness. Cut dough with a 2 1/2-inch biscuit cutter.

Place biscuits close together on a lightly greased baking sheet, careful not to overlap. Brush biscuits melted butter.

Bake in a 425 oven for 10 to 15 minutes or until golden brown. When they come out of the oven brush them on top with a little melted butter.

Serve them right away while they are still piping hot!

Banana Bread

Ingredients:

3-4 ripe bananas
2 cups flour
1/2 stick softened, room temperature butter
1/4 cup of buttermilk
1 cup sugar
2 Eggs (beaten)
1 teaspoon vanilla extract
1/2 teaspoon salt
1 and ½ teaspoon baking soda

Directions:

Preheat the oven to 350°F:
Butter a 9x5-inch loaf pan.

In a medium sized mixing bowl, mash the ripe bananas with a fork until completely smooth.

In a separate large mixing bowl, cream the softened butter and the sugar until creamy.

Add eggs one at a time.

Add mashed bananas.

In a separate bowl, mix the dry ingredients: baking soda, salt and flour.

In a mixing cup, combine the wet ingredients: vanilla extract and the buttermilk and stir.

Add the dry ingredients to the large mixing bowl alternating with the cup of wet ingredients. Mix until combined careful not to over mix.

Pour the batter into the prepared loaf pan.

Bake for 55 to 60 minutes at 350°F. Bread is done when a knife inserted in the middle of the bread comes out clean. If bread is not done, bake an additional 10-15 minutes, checking for doneness at 5 minute intervals.

Allow bread to cool completely on a cooling rack before inverting.

Butter Swim Biscuits

Ingredients:

2 1/2 cups flour
2 cups buttermilk
1 stick butter
4 tsp baking powder
1 tablespoon sugar
1 teaspoon salt

Directions:

Preheat oven to 450 degrees.
Combine all of the dry ingredients in a medium sized bowl.

Next, add the buttermilk and mix all of the ingredients together until a moist dough is formed.

Melt the stick of butter in a microwave safe bowl, and then pour it into an 8x8 or 9x9 baking dish. Make sure that your pan is not too shallow so that the butter doesn't drip out of the pan while it's baking.

Place the dough right on top of the melted butter and use a spatula to spread it evenly across the pan until it touches the sides.

Cut the unbaked, butter-covered dough into 9 even squares.

Bake for 20-25 minutes or until golden brown on top.

Chapter 7

Misc.

Black Eyed Peas

Ingredients:

3 medium smoked ham hocks or 1 smoked turkey leg
1 pound dried black-eyed peas
Onion powder
Garlic powder
Black pepper
Sugar
Lawry's Seasoned Salt
Butter
Vegetable oil
1 chicken bouillon cube

Directions:

Sort and rinse the peas.
Soak peas in a large container with enough cold water to completely cover the peas. Cover with aluminum foil and refrigerate over-night.

When ready to cook the peas, thoroughly rinse, drain and set aside. Place the meat in a pot and add 1 teaspoon of Lawry's Seasoned Salt, 1 teaspoon black pepper, 2 teaspoons garlic powder 2 teaspoons onion powder,
Bring to a boil then lower heat and cook for 1 and 1/2 to 2 hours. Add the drained peas to the pot of cooked ham hocks or turkey. Place pot over medium heat, bring to a boil, reduce heat and cook for 45 minutes. Reduce heat to a simmer, and Add 1/2 stick of butter, 2 tablespoons vegetable oil, 1 tablespoon sugar, 1 chicken bouillon cube. Continue simmering until the peas are tender and the meat is almost falling off the bone. Taste and correct seasoning if needed.

*Note: You can use this recipe for similar types of legumes such as Pinto, Navy, Great Northern, and Lima Beans. Cooking time may vary

Home-Made Chicken Stock

Ingredients:

3-4 chicken thighs
1 large onion (rough chopped)
1 bell pepper (rough chopped)
4 Stalks of Celery (rough chopped)
1 teaspoon Salt
1 teaspoon Black Pepper
1 teaspoon Onion powder
1 teaspoon Garlic powder
1/2 stick of butter
2 chicken Bouillon cubes
2 quarts water

Directions:

Add 2 quarts of water, chicken thighs and all other ingredients into a fairly large pot.

Bring to a boil over high heat. Once pot is boiling lower heat to simmer until meat and vegetables are tender.

Drain liquid into 3-4 jars with a lid and store in refrigerator until ready for use.

Brown Gravy

Ingredients:

3-6 tablespoons of plain flour seasoned with 1-2 teaspoons each of salt, black pepper, and onion powder.

1/4 cup of left over bacon drippings or left over pan drippings from fried chicken or fried pork chops.

Beef Broth.

Directions:

Heat the drippings in a large pan. Be careful not to let it burn, (especially if there are leftover crumbs from frying chicken or pork chops).

When the drippings are hot, slowly and carefully add the seasoned flour a little at a time while constantly whisking. Keep whisking until the flour is the color you desire.

Next, gradually whisk in the beef broth.
Continue whisking.

Keep adding and whisking in the broth until you achieve the thickness you desire. (Continuous whisking will prevent lumps).

Remove the pan from heat, taste and adjust your seasoning.

Fried Okra

Ingredients:

12 ounces fresh okra cut into 1/2 inch pieces
1/2 cup flour
1 cup yellow cornmeal
1 teaspoon black pepper
1 teaspoon salt
Vegetable oil for frying

Directions:

In a medium sized bowl, whisk together the flour, cornmeal, salt and black pepper.

Pour approximately 2" of oil into a pan and heat until hot.

Drain the okra well, then dredge in the cornmeal mixture, remove excess breading and fry until golden brown.

Place on paper towels to drain.

Fried Green Tomatoes

Ingredients:

3-4 green tomatoes cut into 1/4 inch slices
2 large eggs (beaten)
1 cup of buttermilk
1 cup flour
1 and 1/2 cups yellow cornmeal
2 teaspoons black pepper
2 teaspoons salt
Vegetable oil for frying

Directions:

In a medium sized bowl, beat together the eggs with the buttermilk until well combined.

In a separate bowl, whisk together the flour, cornmeal, salt and black pepper.

Pour approximately 2" of oil into a pan and heat until hot.

Drain the tomatoes well, and then dredge them in the egg and buttermilk mixture, then in the cornmeal mixture.
Shake off excess and fry until golden brown.
Place on paper towels to drain.

Salmon Croquettes

Ingredients:

(1) 15 ounces canned salmon
½ cup flour
½ cup yellow cornmeal
½ medium onion, diced
1 large egg, beaten
½ teaspoon Lawry's Seasoned Salt
½ teaspoon black pepper
½ teaspoon garlic powder
½ teaspoon onion powder
¼ cup mayonnaise
Vegetable oil for frying

Directions:

In a large bowl, whisk together flour and cornmeal.

Add salmon, onions, and all other seasonings. Add mayonnaise and beaten egg. Mix until well combined.

Shape the mixture into patties. Heat 2" of oil in a large skillet over medium high heat.

Once skillet is hot fry patties for 2-3 minutes on each side or until they are golden brown.
Allow to drain on paper towels before serving.

Deviled Eggs

Ingredients:

12 eggs boiled and peeled
4 teaspoons sweet pickle relish
4 tablespoons mayonnaise
4 tablespoons yellow mustard
1/2 teaspoon black pepper
1/2 teaspoon salt
1/2 teaspoon sugar
Paprika for garnishing

Directions:

Once the eggs are boiled and peeled, slice them lengthwise and scoop out the center yolks.

In a bowl combine egg yolks with all other ingredients except paprika and mash them with a fork. Spoon filling into egg halves.

Garnish eggs with paprika if desired.

Grits

Ingredients:

2 cups milk
2 cups of water
½ teaspoon salt
¼ teaspoon black pepper
1 cup of quick-cooking grits
1/2 stick of butter

Directions:

Bring milk, water, and salt to a low boil over medium heat. Lower heat and slowly add grits while whisking to avoid lumps.

Cook grits covered over medium-low heat, stirring frequently.
Remove from heat and stir in butter. Season with salt and black pepper.

For Cheese Grits: Add shredded cheddar cheese after grits have been cooked but are still on the stove. Stir constantly until the cheese is fully melted and the grits are smooth.

For Shrimp and Grits: Sauté the shrimp separately and add on top of the cooked grits.

Air-Fried Hamburgers

Ingredients:

Preheat an air fryer to 400 degrees
1 pound ground chuck
1/2 stick melted butter
1 tablespoon beef base (such as Better than Bouillon)
1-2 teaspoons black pepper
½ teaspoon Lawry's Seasoned Salt
1 teaspoon onion powder
1/2 teaspoon garlic powder

Directions:

Whisk together warm melted butter and other seasonings into a bowl. Form meat into patties . Dip patties into the melted butter mixture. Spray the rack of the air fryer with cooking oil. Place the patties in the air fryer.

Fry patties for 5 minutes, flip and fry for an additional 5 minutes.

Hush Puppies

Ingredients:

1 cup cornmeal
1/2 cup of flour
1 tablespoons sugar
1/2 teaspoon baking soda
1/2 teaspoon baking powder
1/4 teaspoon cayenne pepper
1/2 teaspoon salt
1 teaspoon black pepper
1 cup buttermilk
1 large egg, beaten
1 onion (finely chopped)
Vegetable oil for frying

Directions:

Combine the cornmeal, flour, sugar, baking powder, baking soda, salt, black pepper and cayenne pepper in a large mixing bowl.

In a separate bowl, whisk together the egg, and buttermilk. Add it to the dry ingredients along with the chopped onion and its stir until combined.

Heat 2" of oil in a large skillet. When the oil is hot, drop several tablespoons of batter into the hot oil. Do not overcrowd the skillet.

Fry until the hush puppies are golden brown on one side, then flip.
When the hush puppies are done, transfer them to a paper towel to drain.

Peach Cobbler

Ingredients:

Ingredients for the pie filling:

3 (29 oz.) cans of peaches in lite syrup
1 stick of butter
1 cup sugar
1/2 teaspoon cinnamon
1 teaspoon nutmeg
1 tablespoon vanilla extract
3 teaspoons flour.

Directions for the pie filling:

Drain two of the cans of peaches and add just the peaches into a large pot. Place the remaining can of peaches along with the 1 stick of butter in a separate large pot over medium heat and allow everything to melt together.

Once the butter completely melts, stir in the sugar, cinnamon, nutmeg, and vanilla and allow the pot to come to a boil.

Once the pot is boiling, remove 3 tablespoons of peach syrup from it and place in a small bowl. Whisk the 3 teaspoons of flour into the small bowl of peach syrup until completely combined creating a slurry then stir it back into the pot of peaches.

Cook an additional 30-40 minutes or until the syrup thickens. Then remove it from the stove and allow it to cool. It will continue to thicken while you make your pie crust.

Ingredients for the pie crust:

2 ½ cups flour
2 teaspoons sugar
1 teaspoon salt
2 sticks butter cut into cubes
½ cup very cold water
1 egg beaten with 1 teaspoon of water. (This will be used for the egg wash).

Directions for the pie crust:

In a medium sized bowl, add the flour, sugar and salt and whisk together to combine.

Next add the butter cubes to the flour and using your pastry cutter, cut the butter into the flour mixture until crumbs appear.

Slowly add the cold water into the flour until a ball of dough forms. Start with ½ cup and add more water if you need it. Knead the dough quickly to bring it together. (Don't worry if there is flour left in the bowl).

Remove the dough from the bowl, cut into 2 sections and round into balls. Cover each ball tightly with plastic wrap and place in the refrigerator for 35-45 minutes to rest.

Assemble the cobbler:

Preheat oven to 375 degrees.

Remove the dough from refrigerator and add a bit of flour to a working surface or clean counter and place dough on it. Unwrap one ball of dough.

Using a rolling pin, roll the dough out to about ⅓ inch thickness and place on the bottom and up the sides of a 9×13 inch baking pan.

Using a slotted spoon, remove just the peaches from the pot and spoon on top of the dough. Next pour the remaining syrup into the peaches. The mixture will continue to thicken while it is baking.

Roll out the final dough ball and place it on the top of the peach cobbler either as a lattice or as one piece.
Brush the top of the dough with the egg wash then sprinkle lightly with the ground cinnamon.

Bake for 40-45 minutes or until the crust is golden brown.
Let pie cool before serving.

Vanilla Pudding
Ingredients:

3 cups whole milk
3 tablespoons cornstarch
1/4 teaspoon salt
1 cup sugar
4 egg yolks
1 tablespoon butter
2 teaspoons vanilla extract

Directions:

In a small bowl, whisk together ¼ cup of the milk with the cornstarch. Set aside.

In a medium saucepan, whisk together the remaining milk, salt, and sugar. Heat the mixture over medium heat until it is steaming, do not let it boil.

While the milk heats, whisk the egg yolks in a separate small bowl. Once the milk is steaming, slowly stream ½ cup of the hot milk mixture into the egg yolks, whisking constantly..

Slowly add the egg yolk mixture back to the pot, followed by the cornstarch mixture. (This is called tempering) Continue to cook over medium heat, whisking constantly, until the mixture starts to simmer and has thickened.

Remove from the heat and whisk in the butter and vanilla.

Let the mixture cool, cover it with plastic wrap, place it in the refrigerator and allow it to chill for several hours.

Simple Syrup Cake Glaze

Ingredients:

1/3 cup sugar
1/3 cup water
1/8 tsp salt
1 tablespoon flavoring or extract of your choice

Directions:

Add the water, sugar, and salt to a small saucepan.

Bring to a boil and boil just until all of the sugar and salt is dissolved. Remove from the heat.

Add the flavoring or extract and stir to combine. Gently brush on cake that has cooled.

Appendix A

Kitchen Conversions

Dry Measurements

Cups	Tablespoons	Teaspoons	Ounces	Milliliters
1 C.	16 Tbsp.	48 tsp.	8 oz.	237 ml
3/4 C.	12 Tbsp.	36 tsp.	6 oz.	177 ml
2/3 C.	10 & 2/3 Tbsp.	32 tsp.	5 oz.	158 ml
1/2 C.	8 Tbsp.	24 tsp.	4 oz.	118 ml
1/3 C.	5 & 1/3 Tbps.	16 tsp.	3 oz.	79 ml
1/4 C.	4 Tbsp.	12 tsp.	2 oz.	59 ml
1/8 C.	2 Tbsp.	6 tsp.	1 oz.	30 ml
1/16 C.	1 Tbsp.	3 tsp.	1/2 oz.	15 ml

Fluid Measurements

Gallon	Quarts	Pints	Cups	Ounces	Liters
1 gallon	4 quarts	8 pints	16 cups	128 oz.	3.8 liters
1/2 gallon	2 quarts	4 pints	8 cups	64 oz.	1.9 liters
1/4 gallon	1 quart	2 pints	4 cups	32 oz.	.95 liters
	1/2 quart	1 pint	2 cups	16 oz.	480 ml
		1/2 pint	1 cup	8 oz.	240 ml
			1/2 cup	4 oz.	120 ml
			1/4 cup	2 oz.	60 ml
				1 oz.	30 ml

Courtesy of https://www.thehousewifemodern.com/

Appendix B

Stick of Butter Conversions

Sticks	Cups	Tablespoon	Weight oz	Weight grams
1/2 stick	1/4 cup	4 tbsp	2 oz	56.7 g
1 stick	1/2 cup	8 tbsp	4 oz	113.4 g
1 1/2 sticks	3/4 cup	12 tbsp	6 oz	170.1 g
2 sticks	1 cup	16 tbsp	8 oz	226.8 g
2 1/2 sticks	1 1/4 cups	20 tbsp	10 oz	284 g
3 sticks	1 1/2 cups	24 tbsp	12 oz	341 g
3 1/2 sticks	1 3/4 cups	28 tbsp	14 oz	398 g
4 sticks	2 cups	32 tbsp	16 oz	453.6 g

www.foodlovinfamily.com

Appendix C

Cooking Tools for the Handicapped that can be purchased at www.Amazon.com

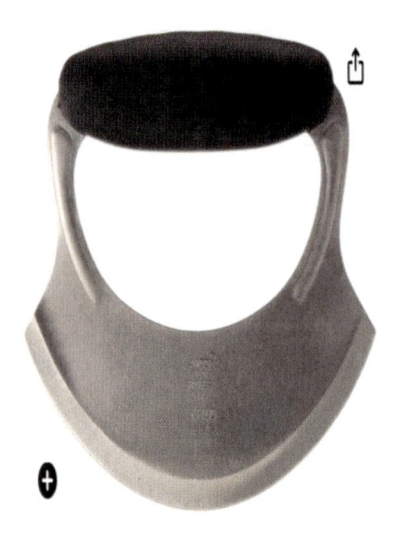

Rocker Knife

Vegetable Chopper

Jar Opener

Instant Pot

Cooking Tools (continued)

Cutting Board

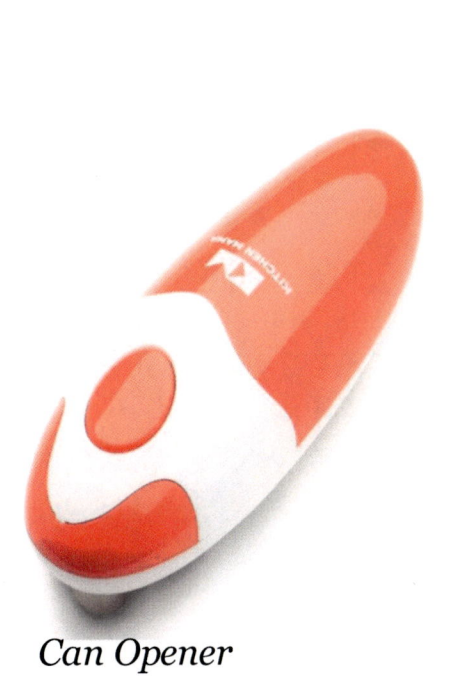

Vegetable and Fruit Peeler

Can Opener

Air Fryer

Appendix D

Cooking Tips

Wash hands thoroughly after handling raw meat to prevent cross-contamination.

Clean up as you go. No one wants to wake up to a sink full of dirty dishes.

Soak meats, especially poultry and pork, in cool water to which a little apple cider vinegar has been added for 15 minutes before cooking to get rid of impurities. Rinse thoroughly afterwards.

Season flour or corn meal with a little salt and black pepper before dredging your meat. This adds flavor to the outside of your meat.

After sorting and rinsing dry beans, soak them in a bowl with enough cool water to cover them. Cover the bowl and place it in the refrigerator overnight. This will make them cook faster and will also reduce Flatulence (gas).

Cooking Tips (continued)

Let meat rest at least 15-20 minutes after cooking to allow the juices to redistribute. This cooking tip will keep it juicy and prevent it from being dry.

Use separate chopping boards for meats and vegetables.

Spread butter on cornbread, biscuits, and rolls immediately after removing them from the oven. This will enhance the flavor.

Add salt to water before boiling pasta. This will add extra flavor.

Turn all pot handles inward on the stove to avoid accidental burns.

To find out if an egg is still safe to eat, do this simple test. Fill a small bowl with fresh, cool water, place the egg in the bowl:

(1) If the egg sinks and falls to its side, it is fresh.

(2) If the egg sinks, but stands upright at the bottom, it is still okay to eat, but you should use it relatively quickly.

(3) If the egg floats, it is no longer safe to eat—it's time to throw it out.

Index

A

Air-Fried Hamburgers	133
Asparagus	44

B

Baked Chicken	30
Baked, Hen (s)	30
Banana bread	118
Banana Pudding	97
Barbecued, Ribs	39
Beef Stroganoff	80
Biscuits, Buttermilk	116
Biscuits, Butter Swim	120
Black Eyed Peas	125
Brown Gravy	127
Broccoli	46
Butter Swim Biscuits	120
Buttermilk Biscuits	116

Index

C

Cabbage, Smothered	48
Cake, Chocolate	104
Cake, Ebony and Ivory	100
Cake, Pound	102
Candied, Yams	56
Catfish, Fried	28
Chef Salad	69
Chicken, Baked	30
Chicken, Fried	20
Chicken Gravy	34
Chicken, Smothered	22
Chicken Noodle Soup	65
Chicken Stock	126
Chili	84
Chocolate Frosting	106
Chuck Roast	35
Chocolate Cake	104
Cobbler, Peach	135
Collard Greens	54
Cornbread	112
Cornbread Dressing	86
Cornbread, Hot Watered	114
Cornish Hen(s)	30
Crust, Pie	136

Index

D

Deviled Eggs	131
Dressing, Cornbread	86

E

Ebony and Ivory Cake	100

F

Fried, Catfish	28
Fried, Chicken	20
Fried, Green Tomatoes	129
Fried, Okra	128
Fried, Pork Chops	24
Frosting, Chocolate	106

Index

G

Garden Salad	67
Gravy, Brown	127
Gravy, Chicken	34
Gravy, Turkey	34
Green Beans and Potatoes	52
Greens, Collard	54
Greens, Mixed	50
Grits	132

H

Hamburgers, Air-Fried	133
Hen(s), Baked	30
Hen(s), Cornish	30
Hot water cornbread	114
Hush puppies	134

Index

M

Meringue	99
Mostaccioli	90
Mac n cheese	82
Meatloaf	26
Mixed Greens	50

N

Neck bones and Potatoes	37

O

Okra, Fried	128
Oven Barbecued Ribs	39

Index

P

Peach Cobbler	135
Pie Crust	136
Pie, Sweet Potato	95
Pork Chops, Fried	24
Pot Roast	35
Potato Salad	73
Pound Cake	102
Pudding, Banana	97
Pudding, Vanilla	138

R

Ribs, Barbequed	39
Roast, Pot	35
Rolls, Yeast	110

Index

S

Salad, Chef	69
Salad, Garden	67
Salad, Potato	73
Salad, Tomato, cucumber, and onion salad	75
Salad, Tuna	71
Salmon croquettes	130
Simple Syrup Cake Glaze	139
Smothered, Cabbage	48
Smothered, Chicken	22
Smothered, Turkey Wings	32
Soup, Chicken Noodle	65
Soup, Vegetable	63
Soup, Vegetable Beef	61
Spaghetti	88
Stock, Chicken	126
Sweet Potato Pie	95

Index

T

Tomato, cucumber, and onion salad	75
Tomatoes, Fried Green	129
Tuna Salad	71
Turkey Gravy	34
Turkey Wings, Smothered	32

V

Vanilla Pudding	138
Vegetable Soup	63
Vegetable Beef Soup	61

Y

Yams, Candied	56
Yeast Rolls	110

Made in the USA
Coppell, TX
26 August 2024